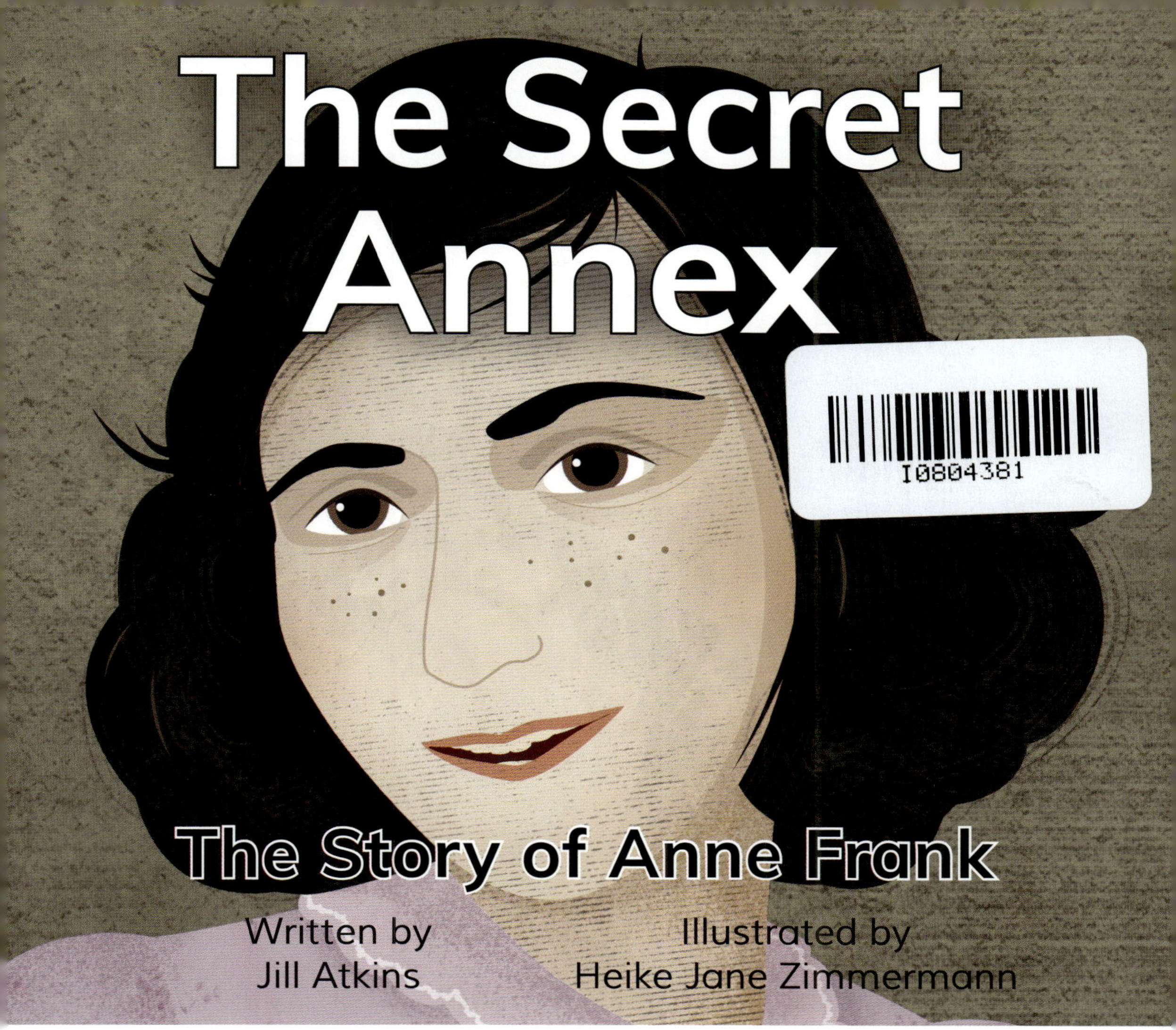

The Secret Annex

The Story of Anne Frank

Written by
Jill Atkins

Illustrated by
Heike Jane Zimmermann

Published in 2026 by
Norwood House Press
2544 Clinton Street
Buffalo, NY 14224

Printed in the United States of America

Library of Congress Cataloging-in-Publication Data:
Names: Atkins, Jill (Children's author). | Rickard, Stephen, 1957-, author. | Zimmermann, Heike Jane, illustrator.
Title: The secret annex / written by Jill Atkins, illustrated by Heike Jane Zimmermann. Where are all the little grey men? / by Stephen Rickard.
Description: Buffalo, NY : Norwood House Press, 2026. | Series: Phonics all-stars: phase 5c
Identifiers: ISBN 9781978578685 (pbk.) | ISBN 9781978578692 (library bound) | ISBN 9781978578708 (ebook)
Subjects: LCSH: Reading–Phonetic method–Juvenile literature. | English language–Phonetics–Juvenile literature. | Frank, Anne, 1929-1945–Juvenile literature. | Extraterrestrial beings–Juvenile literature.
Classification: LCC LB1573.3 A796 2026 | DDC 372.465–dc23

CPSIA compliance information: Batch #CW26NHP: For further information contact Norwood House Press at 1-800-237-9932.

It was June 12, 1942 – Anne Frank's thirteenth birthday.

One of her presents was a writing book. It had a handsome cover with a little lock on the front.

Anne was delighted. She called the book Kitty.

“I’m going to write a diary,” she told her mother and father.

“Good plan,” said her older sister.

A few days later, Anne began writing.

Dear Kitty, Anne wrote. Life has become rather difficult in Amsterdam.

Since Adolf Hitler's German Army had invaded Holland, there were strict new rules for Jewish people to follow.

As her family was Jewish, Anne and her sister were forced to leave their school and go to a school just for Jewish children.

As time went by, Hitler demanded that Jewish people be arrested and sent away.

Anne had no idea where these people were sent.

Would that happen to her family?

One month later, Anne's father took the family into hiding, in rooms above an office. It was a secret annex in a five-story house, up steep stairs behind a bookcase.

Some family friends became their trusted helpers, getting food and other things they needed.

Anne knew the risks their friends were taking. If they were discovered, they could all be shot!

There were other people hiding in the secret annex, as well as the Frank family.

In her diary, Anne described life in the secret annex:

- how cramped the space was
- how there was a second family, with a boy called Peter, hiding there too
- how they couldn't light a fire or use lights at night, because it might give them away

She described exactly how she was feeling too.

The offices downstairs were in use in the daytime, so everyone had to remain silent. Even their footsteps might give them away!

Anne passed the time writing, studying, and making friends with Peter.

How must it have felt to be cooped up like that, day after day, not going out or making a noise?

There were no TVs, computers, or internet then!

All this came to an abrupt end on August 4, 1944, when the secret annex was raided.

Everyone was arrested and transported to a prison camp.

After a few days, some of the helpers went back to the hiding place and found Anne's diary.

They took it to keep it safe.

Sadly, Anne died in a prison camp in March 1945. She was 15 years old.

Her mother and her sister both died in the camp as well.

In her diary, Anne had written, I want to go on living even after my death.

How could she know that this would come true through her amazing diary?

Where Are All the Little Gray Men?

By Stephen Rickard

If we look up into the sky, out beyond our own planet, are there any living things out there?

Or are we all alone in the cosmos?

If there are other living things out there, why haven't we met them?

Where are they all?

The space ships that humans have are not very powerful, so we cannot travel far into space.

So, if we do meet some little gray men, they will need to visit us. They will need to come here to say hello.

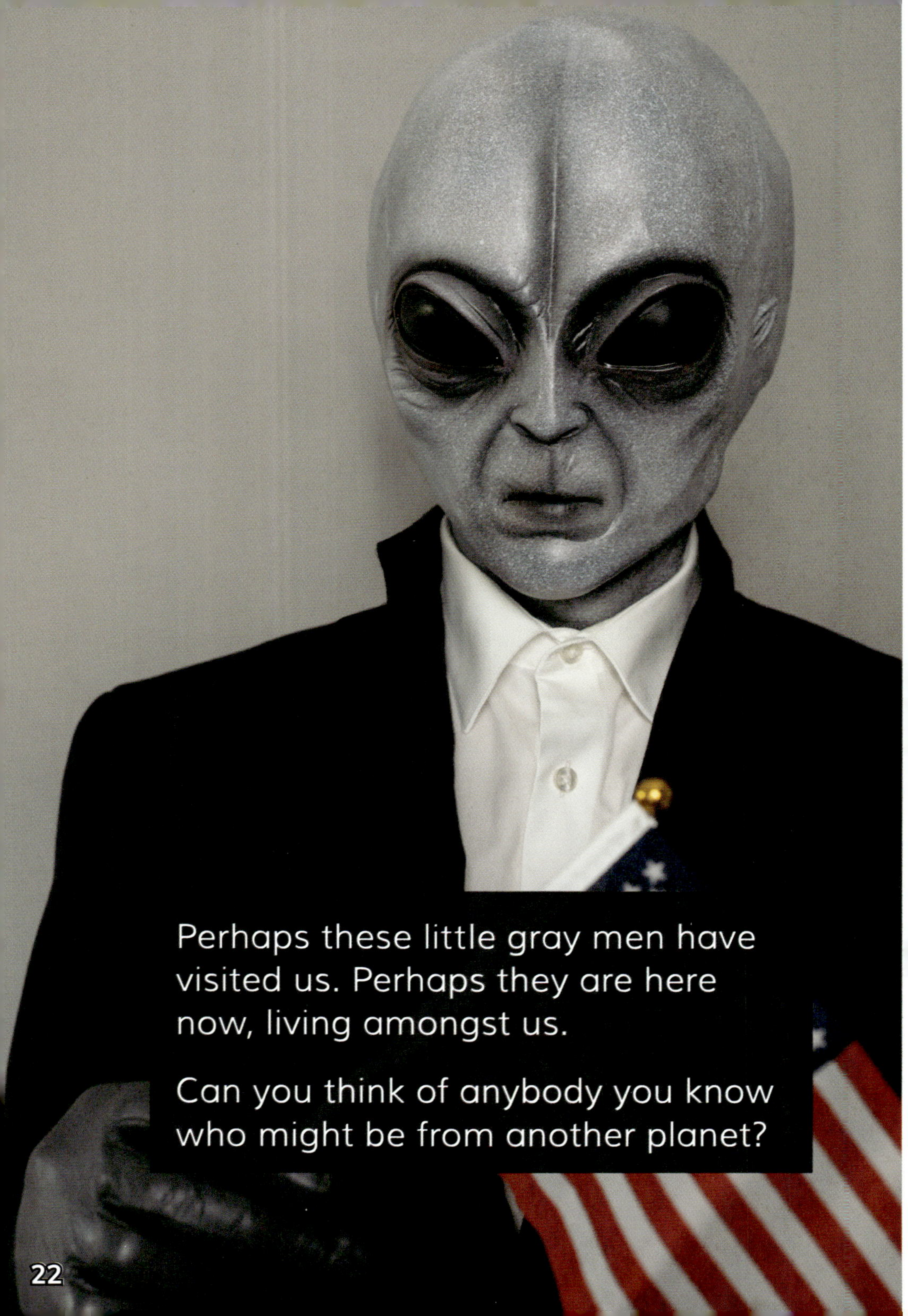

Perhaps these little gray men have visited us. Perhaps they are here now, living amongst us.

Can you think of anybody you know who might be from another planet?

we never see them.

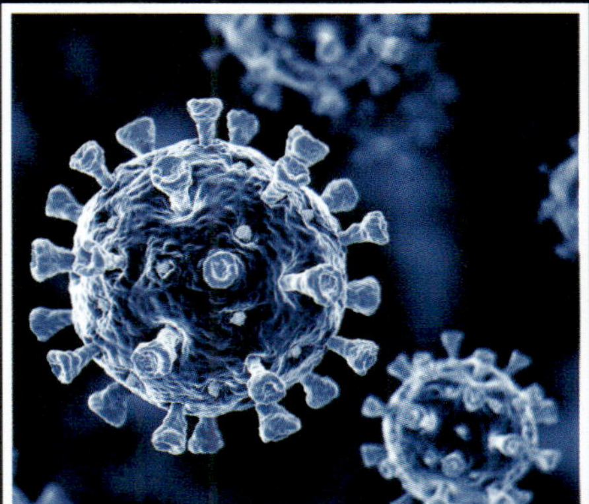

Or perhaps they are here, but they are tiny. Could they be the size of a virus?

Little gray men could visit us in a spaceship, but there might be a few problems.

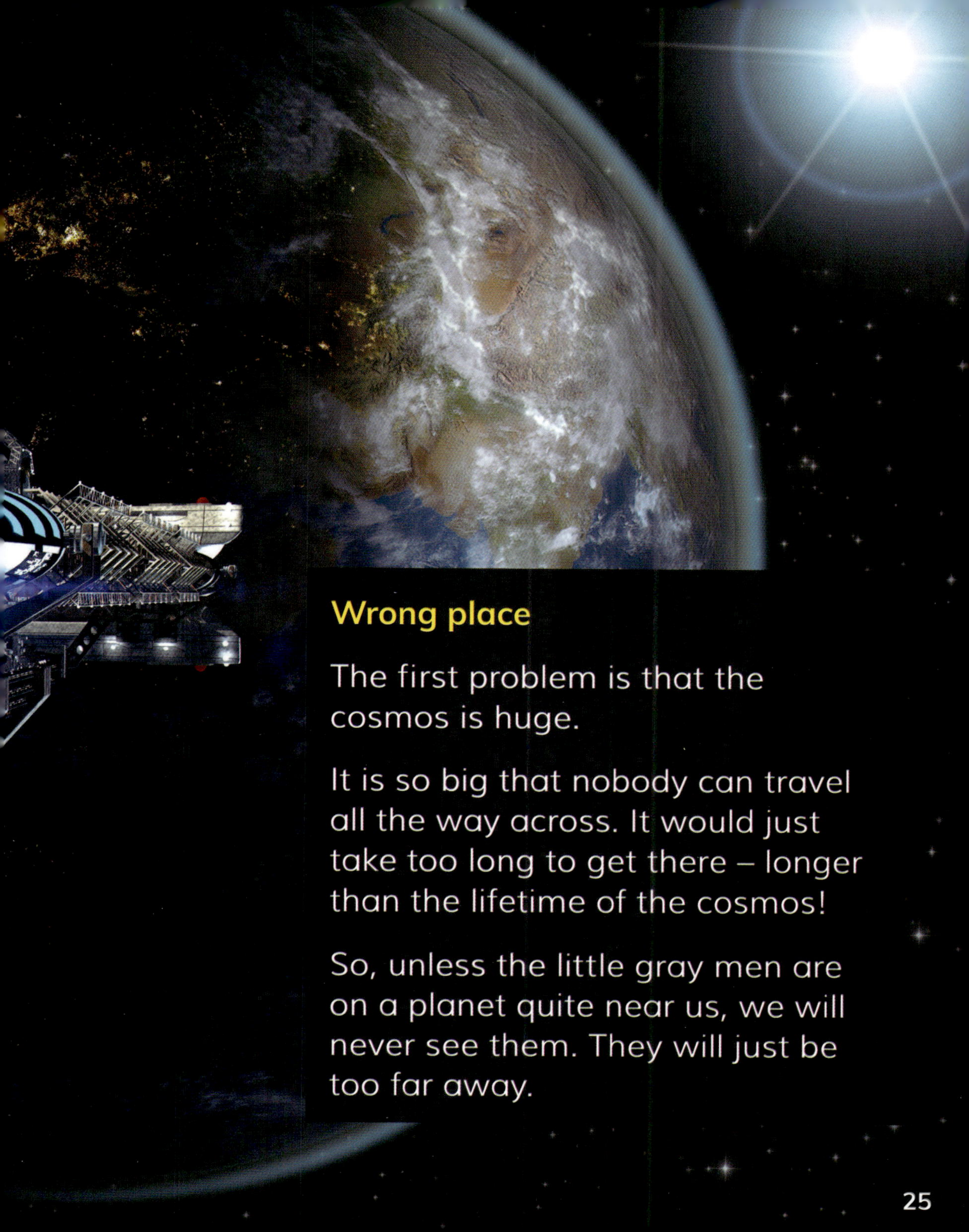

Wrong place

The first problem is that the cosmos is huge.

It is so big that nobody can travel all the way across. It would just take too long to get there – longer than the lifetime of the cosmos!

So, unless the little gray men are on a planet quite near us, we will never see them. They will just be too far away.

Some people think that we could make a shortcut to get from one side of the cosmos to the other. These shortcuts through space are like holes in the cosmos.

They think that a hole in the cosmos like this might connect one part of the cosmos with a different part, so you could travel from one place to the other very quickly.

Do these holes exist? We have no idea!

Wrong time

The second problem with little gray men visiting us is that the cosmos is very old. We think it started with the Big Bang, about 13,800,000,000 years ago.

Our own planet has only been here for about a third of that time, and humans didn't arrive until about 100,000 years ago.

So, for most of the life of the cosmos, humans have not been here.

So, we can only meet the little gray men if they are in the right place **and** at the right time.

It feels as if meeting us would be sheer luck!

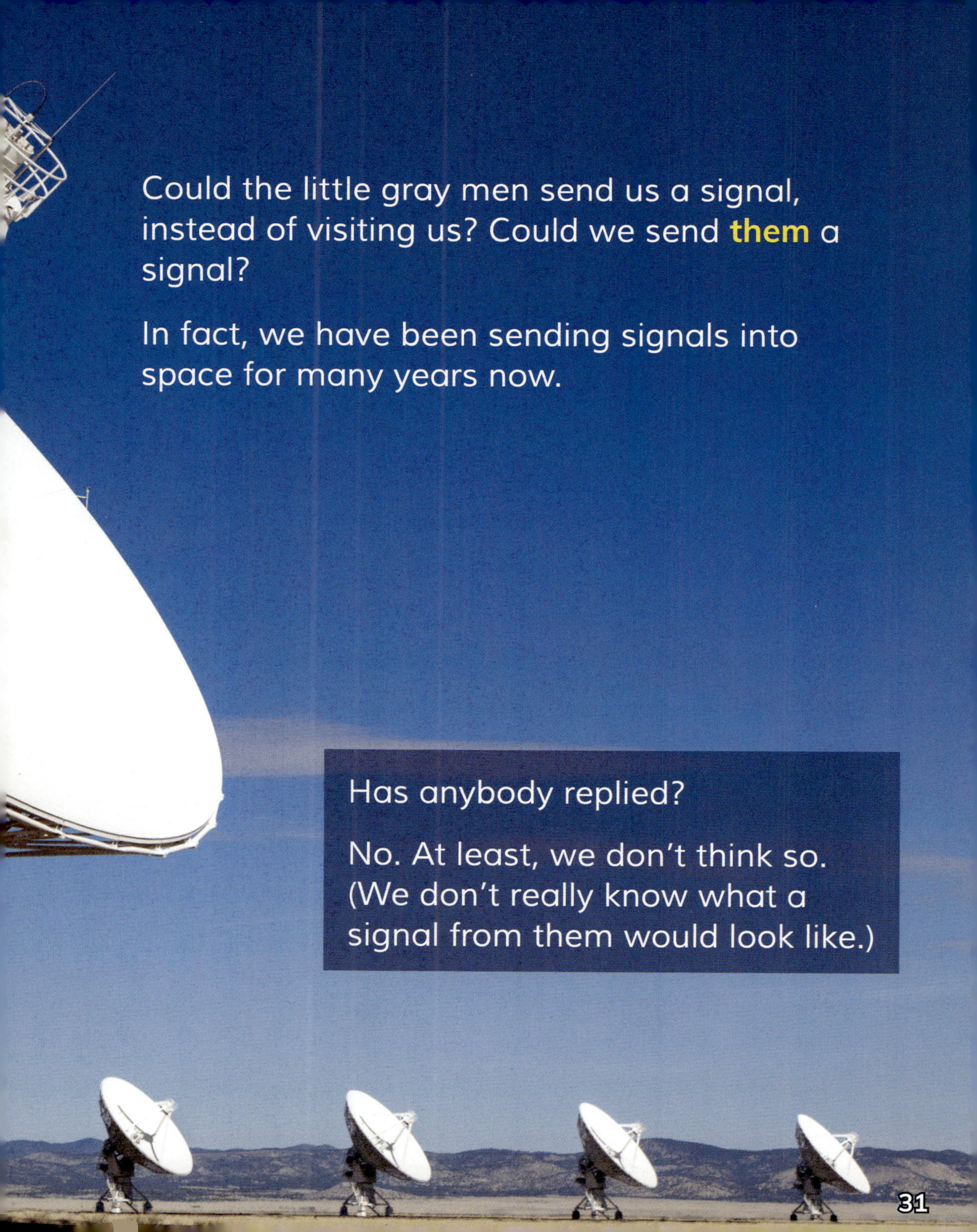

Could the little gray men send us a signal, instead of visiting us? Could we send **them** a signal?

In fact, we have been sending signals into space for many years now.

Has anybody replied?

No. At least, we don't think so. (We don't really know what a signal from them would look like.)

If little gray men did visit us, would they greet us as friends – or would they just attack us?

Do we **really** want to meet little gray men?